POETIC LICENCE IN
A TIME OF CORONA

CHRIS
FITZPATRICK

POETIC LICENCE IN A TIME OF CORONA

TWENTY
FIRST
CENTURY
RENAISSANCE
21CR.IE

Published in May 2022
by 21st Century Renaissance,
The Glasshouse, Harbour Court,
George's Place, Dun Laoghaire,
Dublin A96 P0A4, Ireland

www.21cr.ie

First edition

Copyright ©Chris Fitzpatrick 2022

The moral right of the author, Chris Fitzpatrick, has been asserted.
No part of this publication may be reproduced in any form or by any
means without the prior permission of the publisher.

British Library Cataloguing in Publication Data A catalogue record
for this book is available on request from the British Library

978-0-9927368-8-0

The text of this book is composed in Bodoni

Cover design & layout
Garrett Bennis | garrett@be-creative.ie

Printed in Ireland by ProPrint,
66A Upper George's Street,
Dun Laoghaire, Co. Dublin

ACKNOWLEDGEMENTS

My thanks to Maureen Browne and David Hickey for their encouragement and support; to Richard M. Berlin for his long-distance literary mentorship and friendship; to Professor Mary Horgan (President of the Royal College of Physicians of Ireland and Consultant in Infectious Diseases at Cork University Hospital) for her collaboration on two poems (on pages 6 and 24); and to Alison Hackett for her immense patience and skill.

Some of these poems have appeared before in various print and online versions/formats (as poems, letters, videos); acknowledgements are made to the following: The Irish Times, Sunday Independent, Irish Independent, Business Post, Honest Ulsterman, United We Stand, Medical Independent, The Consultant, dotMD, Psychiatric Times (Any Good Poem), Royal College of Physicians of Ireland (Pause for a Poem), University College Dublin (Poetry in Lockdown: A Pandemic Archive).

A version of the poem about George Blake was read to him shortly before he died in Moscow on December 26th, 2020; he was 98 years of age.

Two poems arose out of conversations I had with my brother, Declan, in the weeks leading up to his death on October 12th, 2021 – and another was prompted by a letter written by Jürgen Klopp to him; these poems are dedicated to Declan.

The poem set on Christmas Day 2021 was inspired by the launch of the James Webb Space Telescope by NASA.

Finally, I would like to acknowledge Sylvia Plath whose poetry means most to me.

for Trish (who usually doesn't like poetry)

All shall be well, and all shall be well,
and all manner of things shall be well.

        Julian of Norwich (1342–1416)

in a time of corona

Lethal attachment
malware for humans
who dreamed you up?
bats? scientists?

Our humanity
is our best immunity
let this go viral

Day shift on now
midwife puts on PPE
baby cries, the same

humongous signs
everywhere, Covid-19
no visitors

do rounds, discharge home
afternoon: phone-call clinic
read algorithms

login on laptop
webinar update
a thousand doctors

catch the news
getting closer to the surge
flatten the curve

wash hands, cough in the
crook of your elbow, keep
apart, stay at home

not enough PPE
battles fought in ICUs
on wards everyday

everything's shut
flick on a comedy channel
tonic I need

phone my mam & dad
they're cocooned & praying hard
without mass

There is a part of me concealed
that is forever England's to hold.
It moves in some stranger through
London's streets plumbed & sealed;
needs no passport to live in its abode
lets me walk with a lighter load.

Daffodils, tulips
yellow blaze outside window
Van Gogh would paint these

blue tit on feeder
bird of paradise come
to visit

spider, skydiver
from ceiling on silken thread
lands softly, runs

midges suspended
in light are a shimmering
gossamer

still canal water
dusk, swans drift on
reflections

in the silvery
moonlight, I dream
wishes come true

First day back
"great to see you"
muffled through masks

on this front-line, all
are troops & casualties
my patient could be me

no time to dwell, just
stick to the rules, protect your
patient & yourself

I don & doff the
PPE, a trainee shows me
she has my back

no hierarchy, work
as one, together but
socially apart

no visitors, just
patients & us, we
quickly acclimatise

trusted wisdoms no
longer apply, we learn fast
share everything

isolation brings
fear in ICU & at home
we are with you

between lungs on
chest X-rays & CT scans, I
see a person's heart

surreal comes nowhere
near, I struggle
to find words

everywhere I look
I see determination
we will get through

as I write this
airplanes are landing
with PPE for us

This morning Anna Akhmatova read my mind.
She knows if I'm happy or sad; picks a poem
for me. Kind, generous, far from dead, she glides
through Parisian salons in my head.

Modigliani drew her over & over,
sometimes stoned, sometimes sober.

There's just something about Anna Akhmatova:
sitting at a table, lying on a sofa – spice of life,
sparkling tonic, making dissonance harmonic.

Azure sky
yellow & red flowers
trees are bright green parasols
we stroll like 19th century Parisians
in dazzling sunlight
(except for the metres apart)
Renoir has come back to paint us
he thinks it's the Bois de Boulogne
he's the one in the straw hat
with the paint brush, by the bandstand

a song thrush sings
"It's a beautiful day
Don't let it get away"

in my reverie
U2 appear, join in
they're the ones in the shades
by the bandstand too

On September 5th, 1971, as a match-programme seller
& ball-boy at the 84th All-Ireland Senior Hurling Final
between Tipp & Kilkenny, I handed a sliotar that had gone
wide to Ollie Walsh for a puck-out in front of a crowd of
sixty-one thousand, three hundred and ninety-three.
The Cats' goalkeeper nodded his head & said "thanks",
despite having let in a rake of goals
(including one between his legs).

That was the game Babs Keating took off his boots & socks
& played in his bare feet & Pat Henderson's hand & hurl
were red with blood (as was the autograph he gave me
after the game).

I remember Croker that day, like it was yesterday:
a sea of blue & gold and black & amber & how the
hair stood up on the back of my neck as I sang
Amhrán na bhFiann with the Artane Boys Band &
the 61,393 all around me.

Dev was there too
& I believed in him
just like I believed in God.

On the night Amy Winehouse
came from London
to sing the blues in Dingle
she bared her soul &
touched my heart
in the small Church of St. James
on the tip of the peninsula
& afterwards on the street
& in the hotel & at the bar

"We only said goodbye with words
I died a hundred times"

when Amy sang the blues
she touched my heart
at the edge of the world
we were never two metres apart

I did not go gently into this good night
I raged & raged against the dying of the light –
little good it did me, I was too far out, beyond saving
when you saw me through the window, I was drowning
not waving

after Dylan Thomas & Stevie Smith

When someone says
"I can't breathe", it's
an emergency
you sit him/her up &
quickly
- call the emergency number
- check the airway
- listen to the chest
- check the saturations
- give oxygen
- put in a line
give
- nebulizers
- antibiotics
- steroids
- diuretics
- more drugs
do
- a swab
- blood tests
- a chest X-ray
you might even need
- a CT
- an anaesthetist
- a bed in ICU
one thing you don't do is
kneel on the person's neck
how could you?

Just when I thought
the beautiful game
had turned its back
on where it came from
the narrow streets
the two-up-two-downs
the high-rises
the five-a-sides on rough concrete
& there weren't
any heroes left
only millionaires with
lucrative sponsorship deals
along comes
Marcus Rashford
twenty-two years of age
graduate of free school meals
& soup kitchens
gifted attacker on the field
fearless defender off the field
comforter of bomb-victims
helper of the homeless
raiser of funds to fight Covid
learner of sign language to judge
a poetry competition for deaf children
advocate of Black Lives Matter
campaigner for free school meals
for hungry children
it's like when they turn on the floodlights
only it's different

Summer, west Kerry
hedgerows dripping with fuchsia
hum of honeybees

Corvids: 19 rooks in a tree

Who are these aliens?
did not invite them
spaceship lit up the night
made the dog bark

monsters
no mouths, no noses
hands blue & sticky
no fingernails

spray chemicals
read minds
take money & clothes

go away

In the photograph, a young man & young woman are sitting with their backs to a mirror in a bar. Maybe it's Paris, or London, or New York. Who knows? Each has an arm around the other. They're looking into each other's eyes. The woman is smiling. Although I can only see the side of the man's face, I know he's smiling too. They're a little shy, like in a first date. It's an old photograph, so, they're dead now. The man is wearing his best suit. The lapels of his jacket are crinkled. It's his only suit. His cap is pushed back on his head, so he can sit close to the woman. His free hand is resting on the table. He pinches the end of his cigarette tightly. He's bewitched by the woman's beauty. If he's not careful, he's going to knock over his drink. Although it's a black & white photograph, the woman is wearing dark-red lipstick. I can see the back of another woman's head in the mirror. The bar is full. Chatter spills into the room I'm in. A boy is collecting glasses. He's not in the photograph, but I can hear the glasses clinking as he picks them up. The man & the woman can barely hear each other. They lean closer. Someone starts to play the piano. It's out of tune. It looks like the man & the woman are going to kiss. It's not going to be like the kiss in Gustav Klimt's painting – more Bogart and Bergman. They stop in mid-air.

With the SkyView
App on my iPhone
I can identify you
for the first time
in sixty-three years

Cicero & Caesar
got you wrong
you're too small
to be the God of War
you're not even red
you're just an apricot
dot a gazillion
miles away

Ziggy Stardust &
the Spiders lied; they
never came from you
they just fooled us
with their crazy clothes
& hairdos

you know Hilary Swank
is on her way to land
on you with her crew

Swank has a lot on her plate
a spacewalk to fix a broken panel
relationship problems among the crew
her daughter off the rails on earth &
her husband in ICU after brain surgery

at the end of a bad day
Swank looks out the
bedroom window of her rocket
hears Van Morrison's
Into the Mystic
tears well up
hers, ours
she needs this song
more than rocket fuel
to keep her going

Yeats's mask:	My mask:
burnished gold	polypropylene (I'm told)
emerald eyes	Chinese
poetic	hygienic
symbolical	practical
mystical	disposable
think persona	think corona
think Noh	think yes

On the way into work, a stranger stops
(two metres in front of me) & points to
where she has seen a kingfisher. She's
beaming with delight. I thank her.

The bird is perched on a branch
at the riverbank. When it hits
the water, it's a topaz-orange
arrowhead – on fire.

When I leave, the kingfisher
is back on the branch.
As I meet other strangers
walking towards me, I tell them
where the kingfisher is.

Before Covid when she scanned
(if she was a racing car driver
she'd be in Formula One)
she always had time for a quick word
sports, politics, weather
I told her I blamed Neymar
for our sons' dodgy hair cuts
she thinks Irish politicians are the best
& prefers Paddy's to Carnival
I say I'm not sure about either

since Covid, she says nothing
apart from "Cash or Card"

when this is all over, I think I'll tell her
about Brazil's 1982 World Cup captain
Socrates who (legend has it) played for
Shelbourne reserves when he was
a medical student in Dublin
it's a good conveyor-belt story
saved up for after Covid

Mr Cox in the newspaper shop says
George Blake is a communist who
doesn't believe in God, but the word
sounds like communion to me.

The Christian Brother, whose brother fought
against Franco in the Spanish civil war, says
George Blake struck a blow for freedom
against the might of the British empire
& that's why an Irishman helped him escape.
Our class says a prayer before English
grammar the pair will make it safely to
Moscow.

I cut out the photograph of George Blake
from the front page of the Irish Press & glue
it in my scrapbook between George Best &
Bruce Reynolds, the Great Train robber.

When I say "I lay me down to sleep,
I pray to God my soul to keep"
I think of George Blake in a ditch
or an attic, or under floorboards
somewhere in England or Belgium
hiding the way priests did in the old days
when we had the Penal Laws.

I still see that old black and white photograph:
the combed hair parting, the large forehead
the crumpled shirt-collar, the black tie
& the dark eyes.

I think of him cocooned
& send these memories
into the snow.

Dry land within reach
hit by a massive wave, all
hands on deck, hold fast

this time we have charts
know where the hidden rocks are
we keep the sails up

batten down the hatches
keep the pumps going
plot our course

below deck, we
care for patients
our most precious cargo

we mourn lives lost in
the surge, heartbreak is
a burden we bear too

exhaustion, we deal
with later, we signed
up for this

at breaking point, we
will not break, this ship will not
go down

The poem is a wound I cut
on myself, deeply I must go
do not ask me the reasons why
I will be the last to know
you are my assistant
please keep your hands steady
if I need gas or ligature
you must be ready
in the distance, I see it!
look! my beating heart!
if I die on this table
you have played your part

for Sylvia Plath

I'm walking along the riverbank
with my dog listening to Hilary
Mantel's Wolf Hall Trilogy on
my phone with my new cancel-the-
sound-of-the-outside-world wireless
headphones. My dog walks behind me.
The pale winterish sun in front of me
is the one Thomas Cromwell sees.
My footsteps are his. This uneven path
with its tree-roots & puddles are
Putney's cobblestones; you can easily
trip if you're not careful. On the Dodder
ferrymen curse at bargemen & the
bargemen curse back. I can smell
the stench of the tannery & the butcher's
offal. A hooded crow crosses my path;
damned cutpurse! I check my wallet;
zip my pocket. I worry for my master;
the knives are out for Wolsey. I pray he
will succumb to excess before they get him.
I advise the king to be more careful; I must be
more careful. Anne is less naïve than everyone
thinks; she has a streak of ruthlessness
I admire. She knows what she wants.
Her pale blue eyes are wide open;

she may lose her head like a martyr
but first she will wear the crown.
She will stop at nothing.
She will let nothing stop her.
She thinks it's worth it to be immortal.
How right she is!
Catherine has powerful allies,
but there are few in this country who will
lift a hand to help her when the time comes.
I will not lift my hand; I have come too far.

The plague is back in London.
It may give me the respite I need, once it does
not kill me. A cormorant appears on the river.
I had not seen him before he dived. He swallows
the fish he has trapped in his jaws. He throws back
his head in exultation. He is Thomas More with
his shabby plumage & his billhook. The poor trout
must have a Tyndale's bible, hidden somewhere

I open the door; the dog barks; I turn on the radio:
more bad news. When I finish Wolf Hall, I'll listen
to Gatsby again. Much as I like her, there's only so
much of Anne I can take. I prefer Daisy in her
immaculate white dress.

Lionel Richie keeps emailing me
& yes, I have to pinch myself
to make sure I'm not imagining it
(I'm not)

I also must be sure it's not a scam
(It's not)

Lionel's photo is on the email
so, the email is from him

the word Hello is written under his picture
– a coded message from "Hello is it me
you're looking for?"

although Diana Ross emails me
with updates of her rescheduled shows
(& don't get me wrong, I appreciate
the trouble she goes to)
Lionel's emails mean the most

Lionel has a big smile in his photo
which makes a change from the emails
I get from the seriously glum people
who email me
(a lot)

Lionel encourages me to keep the faith
because he's coming to St Anne's Park
in June 2022

in the past Lionel has emailed
to apologise over
June 2020 & June 2021

Lionel sounds really upset that Covid
has ruined everything

If Samuel Beckett were here
he'd write Waiting for Lionel Richie

If I had been in Páidí Ó Sé's in 1990 when Dolly Parton
sang Coat of Many Colours & if the man eating the crisps
& the ham sandwich at the bar had turned to me & said
If there was ever such a thing as a pandemic, then you
could be sure one thing, that Dolly Parton would be
the first in the queue to give a million dollars to make a
vaccine, I'd have lifted my glass & said
"Here's to you, Dolly!"

Cyberattack! No
emails. Back to paper &
black Bic biros

bad handwriting is
my firewall. Hackers beware
black Bic biros rule!

Greta Thunberg says
vaccines are a moral test
about thinking of others.

On my phone, a woman
in another world struggles
to catch her breath.

I wonder if what she has
will kill me. I swipe her
away with my finger.

Did my vaccine make
me immune to her?

When I hear Richard M. Berlin
reading Gary Snyder's Mid-August
at Sourdough Mountain Lookout
suddenly I'm back in the front-room
of the small house I grew up in
my father listening to me
reading the only poetry book we have
Songs of a Sourdough by Robert W. Service
my small finger follows the words
on the yellow pages in the dim light
& my small voice says:
"The Northern Lights have seen queer sights
But the queerest they ever did see
Was that night on the marge of Lake Lebarge
I cremated Sam McGee"

Rain on the wind comes
from wherever it blows: Ireland
Finland, anywhere

decades apart we
share memories, grief, joy
old friends go back, pick

up threads where we once
parted, when the world promised
everything, nothing

I think of revolutionary
nights in bars, Marx
on the cover

of Das Kapital
looking up at us
through a rake of pints

last bus gone, the long
walk home, once you
shinned up a pole

declared to the world
beneath its yellow light
something or other

you shook a fist at
the moon, your manifesto
was performance art

immortalised &
metaphysical in a
cyberspace raindrop

in our sixties now
we tread on, thread & tread
pick up, before letting go

shin up that pole once
more; tell me what you see
ahead, more behind

One of my sons converts his bedroom to a gym;
a barbell pounds the floor. In the dining room
beneath, the ceiling rose crashes to the ground
chunks, smithereens everywhere.

In the gaping wound: floorboards,
century-old lime & horse-hair plasterwork,
dangling light flex – a loop of gut.

999 is a friend (who rings a friend who knows a man).

Said man arrives in mask & gloves
takes a history; examines
says the damage is not a reason
to despair
I nod consent to operate.

The clock ticks slowly in the hall
I think the worst
visible scars
battered rose.

"Good as new" he says
 peeling off his gloves like
 they do in Grey's Anatomy.

I look up
he should do
major trauma, face-lifts
nose-jobs.

Afghanistan

a woman begs a soldier
to take her baby

three men cling to a plane
fall from the sky

200,000 deaths; 2 trillion dollars
not a virus; us

If in some smothering dreams you too could pace
behind the hearse we put her in
& in the zipped-up body bag see her worn-out face
her medal of Mary fixed with a safety pin
if you could hear at every jolt along the way
the final moans from her congested lungs
the obscenities of her final day
the pleas for mercy on her innocent tongue
my friend, you could not say we did our best
sacrificed to let others live is a sorry story
an age-old lie – dulce et decorum est
pro patria mori

after Wilfred Owen

Strictly is back! Jive!
Rumba! Tango! Waltz! Salsa!
American Smooth!

In my armchair I
have the lightest step. I know
where my head & my

hips are, at all times.
I skip the news. Wouldn't you for
all this happiness?

My brother says "Go upstairs & find
a book to read when I'm asleep."
His books are neatly arranged:
college, school, teaching notes.
I pick The Tempest; come back downstairs.
"We are such stuff as dreams are made on &
our little life is rounded with a sleep".

No tempest now, only my brother sleeping &
the soft *shush* of his pneumatic mattress –
caressing the silence between us.

Of all the books that you have read
which did you like the most?
I ask, sitting two metres from the bed
in which my brother lies, almost a ghost.
The Remains of the Day, he says. His hoist
nearby, attentive as a butler, eavesdrops.
Slowly, we unwind the clock –
school pullovers I handed down to him,
school-books I'd scribbled on.
I see him on a beach with a bucket & spade;
my mother knitting in the shade.
Life is a book from cover to cover;
at the remains of the day we read back over.

After my brother dies, my dad leads the rosary,
his voice unfaltering through mask & tears.
I close my eyes & see my family kneeling, elbows
on the kitchen chairs, the Sacred Heart picture
over our heads, three children in pyjamas,
homework done, schoolbags packed, ready for bed
& the kingdom come.

His youngest son dead, my dad holds fast.
He's known life's cruelties; never wavers.
Death does not break his trust in crucifix & Saviour.

Back in our old kitchen again:
my brother is seven & I am ten.

I Google images of the virus for a PowerPoint presentation
I copy & paste green spiked shells
click save

on the kitchen table my dad spreads out newspapers
cuts the green spiked shells with the bread knife
& with awl & string makes conkers for us

I examine each in turn – pick the biggest & shiniest
smash five in school next day & not a mark on it
my dad calls it "a real beauty"

Doug is our dog
the glue that sticks
us together in a
world that threatens
to pull us apart
a student of Zen
he's reduced
life to essentials –
walk, food, bed
& a word
that's neither
noun nor verb
to him
but
is him –
love
when I look at him
I say there is
a God to make
such goodness

Just when I
was thinking of
Mariah Carey &
what I want for
Christmas
WHAM!
it's going to
be last
Christmas
this
Christmas
all over again

twenty-seven

    migrants

        drown in the

            English Channel

we say
  "we're all in

    the same boat"

                we're

not

their   dead

    bodies

        float

      on

            my   page

    just

      words

No brain
just a bit
of RNA
smarter
than we
think

sizes
us up
picks
us off
in ones
& twos
& droves

shows
no mercy
knows its
Nietzsche

8 am
News
cases – soaring
hospitals – flat-out
healthcare workers – sick
teachers – sick
children – off-school
hospitality & entertainment – on their knees
PCR tests – run-out; opposition politician: very annoyed
antigen tests – dos, dont's, same old, same old
boosters – vox-pop: long queues, freezing cold, who's next?
Omicron – expert on crackly phone line: concern, no panic
(my aunt just died from Covid in England, RIP)
circuit breaker – audible studio groan
pandemic unemployment payments – continue or stop
(my daughter sends a photo of her Christmas tree)
Omicron – expert back on better phone line: time will tell
back to antigen tests – quick revision
Business – markets volatile
Rugby – Munster players in South Africa test positive
Premiership – Man U going nowhere fast
News Summary (can't hear, kettle on)
Weather – turning more unsettled
(empty the dishwasher; take a chance; hang out the clothes)

When I hear that Paddy Moloney
of the Chieftains has died
I remember our college band
(Dada meets punk meets trad)
split up after one anarchic set
in Theatre L of the Arts Block

For a while afterwards, I used to dream
that Paddy had come on stage
& jammed with us

I digitally remaster –
him & me on the uilleann pipes, final encore:
Sex Pistols, Ramones, jigs, hornpipes,
slow-airs

Winter solstice
my soul is a chamber
filled with light

In a gazillion light years
(if we're lucky) we might
be a micro-dot of infra-red
captured by a giant telescope
orbiting the curved edge of the
universe (where it folds back
on itself in infinite repetitions).

But now is not the time
for this.

The stuffing is perfect. I pulled
the long piece off the Christmas
cracker. Everyone is smiling in
the room & on zoom.

I'm a hermit crab
not a walrus

you'd need to be Kafka
to describe my metamorphosis:
hiding in my shell all day
peeking out when the coast is clear
(eyes-on-stalks)
snatching food awkwardly with my claws
not to mention – the waiting

A son bursts in the door.
"It's over!" he shouts
waving his phone.

A few hours later, a surgeon removes
a cancer from my face. Postponed before,
I'm relieved to get it done.

A nurse says Meat Loaf has died.
"Like a bat out of Hell"
I hum in my head.

In the shopping centre, it feels like
we just qualified for the World Cup.
Ole! Ole! Ole?

I'm walking home in the semi-darkness listening to Joni Mitchell
on my headphones. The footpath is wide; I keep to one side of it.
Two women jogging towards me cross to the other side. There's no
one else around. I keep my head down, eyes fixed
       on the floating moon
              upside down streetlights in the canal.

When I made my confirmation in 1969
the Archbishop asked me how long Christ
had lived on earth. "Christ lived on earth
thirty-three years & lived a most holy life
in poverty & suffering". I rattled off the
green catechism answer. Then the Archbishop
leaned towards me (I could smell his Old Spice)
& slapped me lightly on the cheek & I was
a soldier of Christ. I had a red silk rosette
with a silver medal depicting the Holy Ghost
as a dove on one lapel of my school blazer
& a silver fáinne on the other. That afternoon,
my mam & dad brought me to see Anne of a
Thousand Days. My teacher said Henry VIII
was the kind of Catholic who wanted to have
his cake & eat it. That summer, I went to the
Gaeltacht in Donegal. You could only dance
with the same girl once at a céilí & if you
were caught speaking English or smoking
you were sent home. Because there was trouble
in the north, some of the older boys went on
manoeuvres at night, just in case. On the way
back to Dublin we stopped off to see Oliver
Plunkett's head in the church in Drogheda &
said a prayer the pope would make him a saint.
I remember wondering if Anne Boleyn was a
Protestant saint, given what happened to her,
but I didn't dare ask.

Back then, I knew nothing about the Civil War.
I thought we just beat the Black & Tans & then
there was the Eucharistic Congress & that was it.

Whenever I'm in Paris, one of things I love to do
is to sit in one of the green-painted metal chairs
with the angulated seats by the lake in the
Tuileries gardens
– when I lean back, I see only sky

I bet James Joyce sat here, dreaming
– 1000 copies
        sky-blue wrappers
                Ulysses, a cloud

My brother started supporting Liverpool
when he was seven & I had to give him
half the bedroom walls for his posters.
He also took over the back of the door
& used the mirror for stickers.

When he said his prayers at night, he
used pray out loud for Liverpool which
I put up with because he was younger
& more religious than me.

Soon, he had my mam praying for Liverpool
& she introduced him to candles, novenas
& special intentions: St. Anthony (lost form),
St. Jude (extra time, losing).

When he moved out, he put up a sign on his
new home that said ANFIELD. He had a red car,
a red phone, a season ticket.

When he was very ill, Jürgen Klopp wrote
a letter to him & said "You'll never walk alone".
It was like chemotherapy that worked & had happy
side-effects only.

"You'll never walk alone" was played at his funeral
& is on his headstone.

When Liverpool beat Chelsea 11-10 on penalties
in the Carabao Cup Final, everyone agreed with my
sister-in-law's post-match analysis that my brother
had put in a good word above.

The wooden bridge connects the mainland
to the island. Underneath, the winter sea swells
mercilessly; it will drag me down, suck the life
out of me, given half a chance. The waders show
me the white underparts of their wings & their red
legs. It is not enough. Their songs are just cries.

Ahead of me, a small boy runs: striped T-shirt,
plastic sandals, towel under his arm, togs on
his head. He splashes in the tide. It is summer.

When I catch up with him, he doesn't see me.

When the French writer Colette was eight years
old she thought the word presbytère meant
a little snail with a yellow & black striped shell
& when her mother said the word really meant
la maison du curé, Colette was so upset that,
at first, she wanted the curé, Monsieur Millot,
to be made to live inside the little snail's shell.
Then, in a moment of inspiration, she changed
the meaning of presbytère to describe a secret
place on the terrace wall shaded by lilac trees
which she adorned with little pebbles & pieces
of coloured glass & to her mother's astonishment
called herself le curé sur le mur.

   after Sidone-Gabrielle Colette

in a time of war

Standing in a queue of visitors outside a prison
in the snow during the time of Stalin's terror
a woman with blue lips asked Anna Akhmatova
if she could describe this & the poet said she could
& it took thirty years to publish this poem.

BIOGRAPHY

During the pandemic, Chris Fitzpatrick has worked as a consultant obstetrician and gynaecologist in the Coombe Women & Infants University Hospital, Dublin (where he was Master/CEO 2006 - 2012), as Clinical Lead for Covid-19 Vaccinations in the Dublin Midlands Hospital Group (Health Service Executive), and as a clinical professor in University College Dublin (UCD).

Before studying medicine, he studied English in UCD. Inspired by advice given to him when he was a junior doctor by Oscar laureate Sir Alec Guinness, he developed a special interest in the role of the humanities in medical education and training. He is a Fellow of the Royal College of Physicians of Ireland (RCPI) and clinical lead for RCPI's applied drama collaboration with Ireland's national theatre, the Abbey Theatre. He was co-writer with Ruán Magan of the literary drama, And Spring Shall Come, commissioned by the Royal College of Surgeons in Ireland, and produced by Moya Doherty as part of its centenary commemoration of Easter 1916 and World War I. In 2019 he played the part of a doctor in Mary McGuckian's award-winning feature film, A Girl from Mogadishu, based on the life of Somali-Irish anti-FGM activist Ifrah Ahmed. He has published short stories and poetry and is a regular contributor to newspapers. Poetic Licence in a time of Corona is his first collection of poetry.

In Jan 2020, in Belfast City Hospital, he donated a kidney to an anonymous patient as part of a UK altruistic living donor kidney sharing scheme. He retired from clinical practice as an obstetrician and gynaecologist in December 2021. He is married to Trish; they have four grown-up children, and a dog. His idea of heaven is the Dingle peninsula, Co. Kerry.

**TWENTY
FIRST
CENTURY
RENAISSANCE**
21CR.IE